WOMEN GOT GAME

WOMEN'S PROFESSIONAL HOCKEY

ANNE E. HILL

Lerner Publications ◆ Minneapolis

For Abby Hill, the memories we made in the decade you played hockey are some of my favorites with you. And to your amazing female coaches, especially Mary Restuccia and Cara Morey, for fostering your love of the sport.

Copyright © 2026 by Lerner Publishing Group, Inc.

All rights reserved. International copyright secured. No part of this book may be reproduced, stored in a retrieval system, or transmitted in any form or by any means—electronic, mechanical, photocopying, recording, or otherwise—without the prior written permission of Lerner Publishing Group, Inc., except for the inclusion of brief quotations in an acknowledged review.

Lerner Publications Company
An imprint of Lerner Publishing Group, Inc.
241 First Avenue North
Minneapolis, MN 55401 USA

For reading levels and more information, look up this title at www.lernerbooks.com.

Main body text set in Aptifer Slab LT Pro. Typeface provided by Linotype AG.

Editor: Brianna Kaiser **Designer:** Mary Ross

Library of Congress Cataloging-in-Publication Data

Names: Hill, Anne E., 1974– author.
Title: Women's professional hockey / Anne E. Hill.
Description: Minneapolis : Lerner Publications, 2026. | Series: Lerner sports. Women got game | Includes bibliographical references and index. | Audience: Ages 7–11 | Audience: Grades 2–3 | Summary: "Star hockey players such as Kendall Coyne Schofield and Taylor Heise are leading the way in the PWHL. Sports fans will love learning about the league's amazing history-making moments and its plans for the future"— Provided by publisher.
Identifiers: LCCN 2024039682 (print) | LCCN 2024039683 (ebook) | ISBN 9798765668887 (library binding) | ISBN 9798765683620 (paperback) | ISBN 9798765682296 (epub)
Subjects: LCSH: Professional Women's Hockey League—Juvenile literature.
Classification: LCC GV847.8.P76 H55 2026 (print) | LCC GV847.8.P76 (ebook) | DDC 796.962/640820973—dc23/eng/20241121

LC record available at https://lccn.loc.gov/2024039682
LC ebook record available at https://lccn.loc.gov/2024039683

Manufactured in the United States of America
1-1011984-53859-1/9/2025

TABLE OF CONTENTS

STATE OF HOCKEY 4
FAST FACTS 5

CHAPTER 1
STARTING THE LEAGUE 8

CHAPTER 2
OWNING THE ICE 16

CHAPTER 3
TRAILBLAZERS. 22

GLOSSARY. 30
LEARN MORE. 31
INDEX. 32

STATE OF HOCKEY

The pressure was on as Minnesota took to the ice on May 29, 2024. They faced Boston in the last game of the first Walter Cup finals.

The Walter Cup finals is the championship playoff series of the Professional Women's Hockey League (PWHL). The series is the best of five games. Boston won Game 1, while Minnesota won Games 2 and 3.

Game 4 was 0–0 in double overtime when Minnesota's Sophie Jacques put the puck in the net. With two series wins already, the team celebrated. They thought they had won the Cup.

FAST FACTS

- THE PWHL HAS THREE AMERICAN TEAMS (BOSTON, MINNESOTA, AND NEW YORK) AND THREE CANADIAN TEAMS (MONTRÉAL, OTTAWA, AND TORONTO).

- IN 2023, TAYLOR HEISE MADE HISTORY AS THE FIRST-EVER PWHL DRAFT PICK.

- TORONTO HAD THE BEST RECORD FOR THE FIRST REGULAR SEASON.

- TORONTO'S NATALIE SPOONER LED THE PWHL IN POINTS FOR

Minnesota's Liz Schepers (*number 21*) scoring on Boston during Game 5 of the Walter Cup

Then the goal was called back for goaltender interference. Minnesota forward Taylor Heise had fallen into the net, blocking Boston goaltender Aerin Frankel. The game continued. Boston's Alina Müller scored just over a minute later, forcing the series into Game 5.

Neither team had scored by the beginning of the second period of Game 5. But when the time was right, Sydney Brodt passed to Liz Schepers, who took the shot. Goal! Minnesota had taken the lead.

During the third period, Michela Cava skated behind Boston's goal before making her shot. Another goal for Minnesota! Minnesota got one more goal when team captain Kendall Coyne Schofield scored on an empty Boston net.

After the game ended just over two minutes later, the Minnesota players threw their sticks and gloves in celebration. This time, the win was real. Minnesota had won the first Walter Cup.

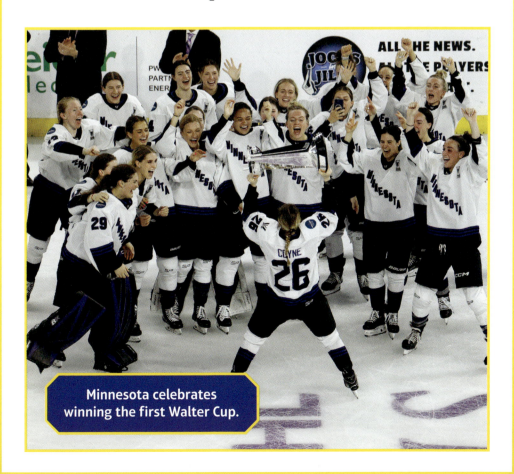

Minnesota celebrates winning the first Walter Cup.

Chapter 1

STARTING THE LEAGUE

Jayna Hefford shoots the puck for Canada in the 1997 IIHF Women's World Championship.

The story of women's pro hockey started 25 years before the PWHL began. It was not an easy journey to create a lasting women's pro hockey league in North America.

In 1999, the National Women's Hockey League began in Canada. But it only had a few western Canadian teams and did not play a regular schedule. The Canadian Women's Hockey League took over in 2007 and ran for 12 seasons. The league did not pay its players a salary—a certain amount of money a person is paid at a regular time. Many of them had other jobs while also playing hockey.

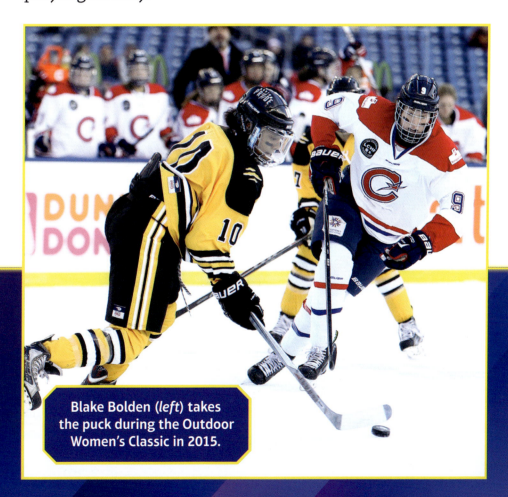

Blake Bolden (*left*) takes the puck during the Outdoor Women's Classic in 2015.

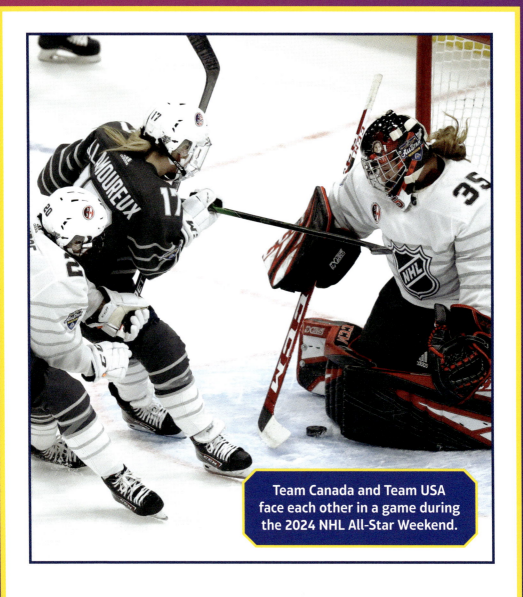

Team Canada and Team USA face each other in a game during the 2024 NHL All-Star Weekend.

In 2020, players in both Canada and the United States created the Professional Women's Hockey Players Association (PWHPA). The group wanted players to receive salaries and be treated fairly. They also wanted teams to have sponsors.

Two years later, the PWHPA partnered with Mark Walter and Billie Jean King to create the PWHL. Walter owns the Los Angeles Dodgers baseball team. King is a former pro tennis player and supporter of women in sports.

TEAM NAMES

During the PWHL's first season, the league's six teams were all named for their location. In September 2024, the PWHL shared the teams' new names: Boston Fleet, Minnesota Frost, Montréal Victoire, New York Sirens, Ottawa Charge, and Toronto Sceptres.

The PWHL began with six teams in locations where women's hockey is popular. The three US teams were Boston, Minnesota, and New York. The three Canadian teams were Montréal, Ottawa, and Toronto.

In September 2023, the six teams took turns choosing players during the first PWHL Draft. Minnesota chose Taylor Heise with the first pick.

Taylor Heise (*right*) shakes hands with Billie Jean King after Heise was chosen with the first overall 2023 PWHL Draft pick.

MOVIE MAGIC

After the 2015 movie *Inside Out*, more girls signed up to play youth hockey. The movie starred Riley, a girl from Minnesota who played hockey. In 2024, *Inside Out 2* came out. Kendall Coyne Schofield of the Minnesota Frost voiced a character in the movie.

Kendall Coyne Schofield at an event for *Inside Out 2* in 2024

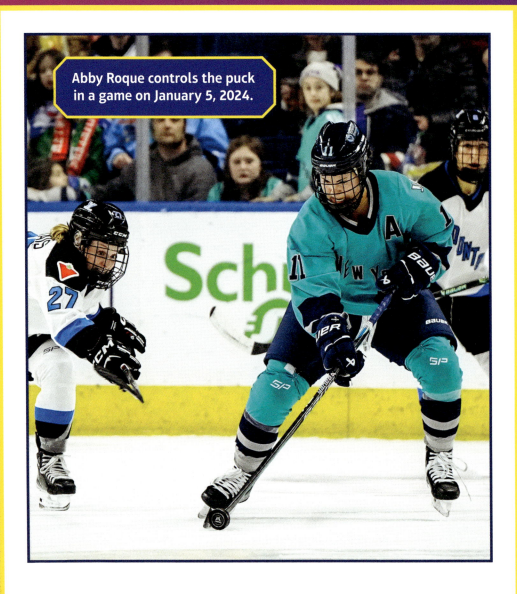

Abby Roque controls the puck in a game on January 5, 2024.

The PWHL began play in January 2024. At the season's end in May, the top four teams moved on to the playoffs to determine the winner of the Walter Cup.

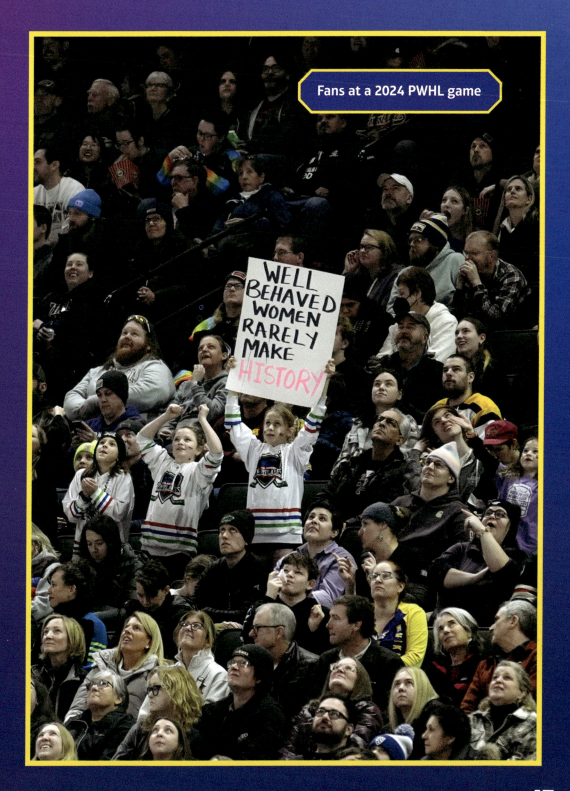
Fans at a 2024 PWHL game

Chapter 2

OWNING THE ICE

On January 1, 2024, New York faces Toronto in the first PWHL game.

The first season of the PWHL began on January 1, 2024. New York faced Toronto in front of a sold-out crowd. Nearly three million people across Canada watched it on TV.

The game was full of firsts and exciting moments for New York. Defender Ella Shelton scored the league's very first goal. Her teammates Alex Carpenter, Jill Saulnier, and Kayla Vespa all scored in the third period. And goaltender Corinne Schroeder had a 29-save shutout. That meant Schroeder saved all the shots made by the other team. Shelton, Carpenter, Saulnier, Vespa, and Schroeder all helped New York win 4–0.

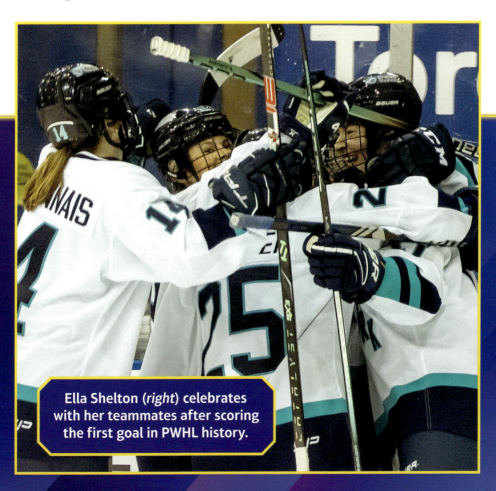

Ella Shelton (*right*) celebrates with her teammates after scoring the first goal in PWHL history.

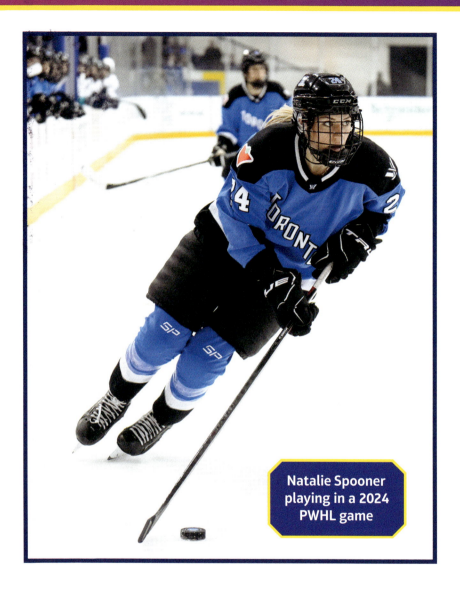

Natalie Spooner playing in a 2024 PWHL game

Toronto had the best record in the first regular season. They had 13 wins, four overtime wins, and seven losses. One reason for their success was their star forward Natalie Spooner. Her scoring helped them win 11 games in a row.

Spooner led the league in points with 20 goals and seven assists in the regular season. She received the first Billie Jean King Most Valuable Player (MVP) award for her amazing season. She was also named Forward of the Year.

AWARD WINNERS

At the end of the first PWHL season, awards were given to some of the league's best players. Montréal's Erin Ambrose was named Defender of the Year, while Toronto's Kristen Campbell was named Goaltender of the Year. Minnesota forward Grace Zumwinkle was named Rookie of the Year.

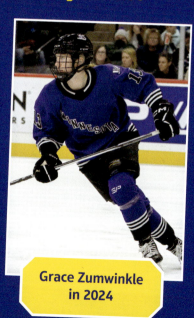

Grace Zumwinkle in 2024

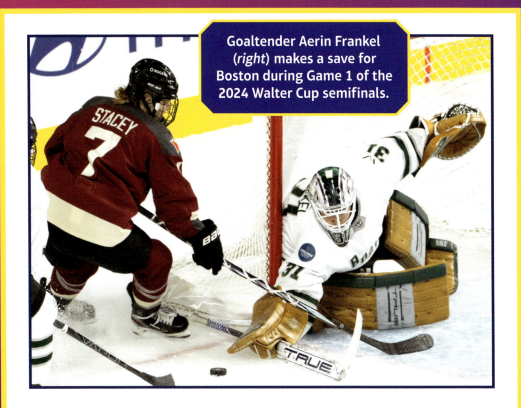

Goaltender Aerin Frankel (*right*) makes a save for Boston during Game 1 of the 2024 Walter Cup semifinals.

During the 2024 Walter Cup semifinals, Boston and Montréal battled to see which team would move on to the finals. Boston won three straight games, all in overtime. Boston took the first game 2–1 in overtime. Susanna Tapani scored the game-winning goal, and Aerin Frankel made a league record 53 saves.

Frankel helped her team again in Game 2, which went into triple overtime. The score was tied 1–1 until forward Taylor Wenczkowski tapped in a pass from defender Sidney Morin. Game 3's overtime lasted for just 62 seconds before Tapani found the back of the Montréal net. Boston won the game 3–2.

DUEL AT THE TOP

On April 20, 2024, 21,105 PWHL fans packed the stands at a sold-out game. Known as Duel at the Top, the game was held at the Bell Centre in Montréal, Quebec. It was the largest crowd ever for a women's hockey game. Toronto beat Montréal 3–2 in overtime.

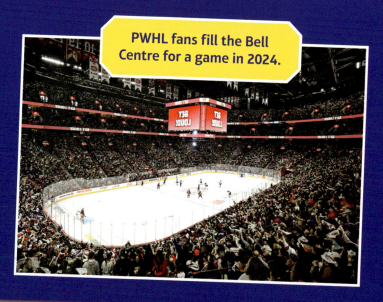

PWHL fans fill the Bell Centre for a game in 2024.

Chapter 3

TRAILBLAZERS

Kendall Coyne Schofield warms up for the 2019 NHL All-Star skills competition.

The PWHL is full of talented players. One of them is Olympic medal winner Kendall Coyne Schofield. The former captain of the US National team is captain of the Minnesota Frost, and she is a member of the PWHL Players Association. This group works for the players to make sure they are treated fairly.

In 2019, Coyne Schofield made history when she skated in the NHL All-Star skills competition, which shows the skills of the best pro hockey players. She was the first woman to compete at the competition. In the first PWHL regular season, Coyne Schofield had six goals and 10 assists. She also had a goal and three assists during the playoffs.

Coyne Schofield scoring in a 2024 PWHL game

Goaltender Kristen Campbell is a big reason why Toronto finished the first PWHL regular season in first place. She saved more than 92 percent of the shots she faced. She also had three shutouts during the regular season and two in the playoffs. This total was more than any other PWHL goaltender.

MAKING SAVES

Aerin Frankel is one of the best goaltenders in the PWHL. She made 455 saves during the first regular season for Boston. She also made 286 saves in the playoffs. Frankel had more saves than any other PWHL goaltender that season.

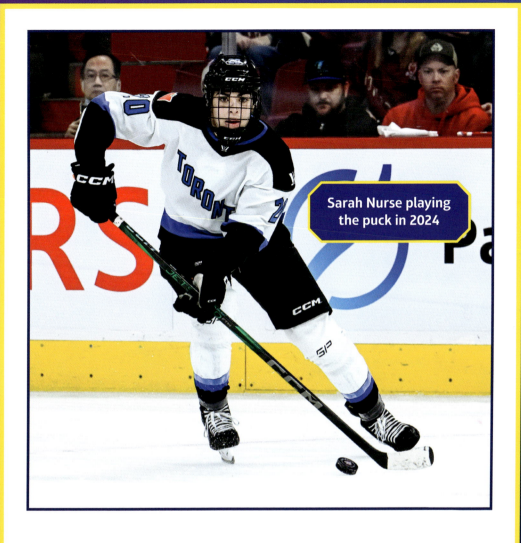

Sarah Nurse playing the puck in 2024

Campbell's teammate Sarah Nurse also helped Toronto. Nurse is an Olympic medal winner. She played four seasons of college hockey for the University of Wisconsin before playing forward for Toronto. She finished the first PWHL regular season with 11 goals and 12 assists. Her 23 points were tied for second-most in the league.

Taylor Heise played college hockey for the University of Minnesota before joining the PWHL. She had four goals and nine assists during the first PWHL regular season. Heise lit up the playoffs with five goals and three assists, helping Minnesota win the Walter Cup. She was named the 2024 PWHL Ilana Kloss Playoff MVP.

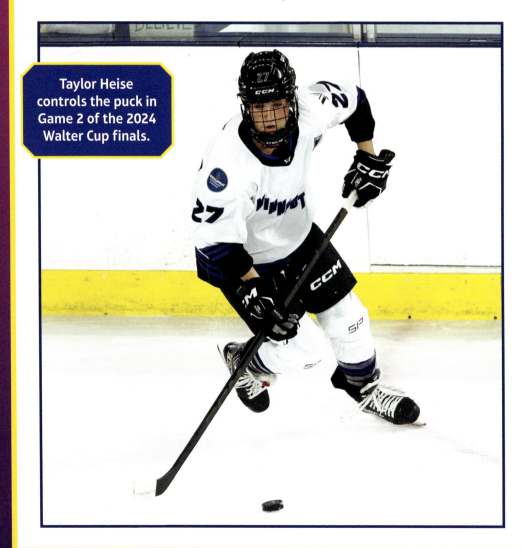

Taylor Heise controls the puck in Game 2 of the 2024 Walter Cup finals.

RISING NEW YORK STAR

Olympic medal winner Abby Roque played four seasons of college hockey for the University of Wisconsin. She helped them win the college championship in 2019. As a forward for the PWHL's New York team, Roque had six goals and seven assists in the first regular season.

In the 2024 PWHL Draft, New York selected Sarah Fillier with the first pick. She had played at Princeton University. Teams chose other well-known players, including Amanda Kessel, Hannah Bilka, and Elle Hartje, in the draft. The PWHL began with players from a dozen countries. As the league grows, players from even more countries will likely join.

Abby Roque in 2024

With millions of fans and young hockey players tuning in to watch the PWHL, the league will likely add more teams in other cities. The league and its stars inspire young hockey players. Fans can look forward to watching the future stars and best moments of the PWHL.

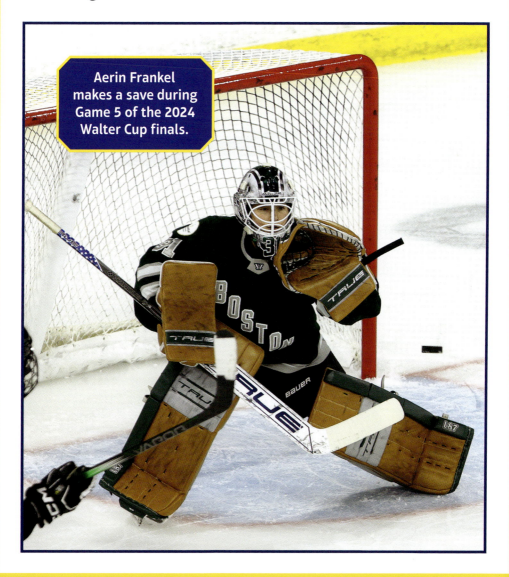

Aerin Frankel makes a save during Game 5 of the 2024 Walter Cup finals.

GLOSSARY

assist: a pass from a teammate that leads directly to a goal

defender: a player whose main job is to stop the opposing team from scoring

forward: a player whose main job is to score

goaltender: a player whose main job is to stop the other team's puck from getting into their goal

overtime: extra time added to a game when the score is tied at the end of the normal playing time

period: one of the divisions of playing time in a game. Hockey has three periods.

playoffs: a series of games played to decide a champion

rookie: a first-year player

semifinal: a game or a series of games coming before the final round in a tournament

sponsor: a person or business who pays for costs of something such as an athlete

LEARN MORE

Duling, Kaitlyn. *Women in Hockey.* Lake Elmo, MN: Focus Readers, 2020.

Goldstein, Margaret J. *Meet Sarah Nurse: Olympic Hockey Superstar.* Minneapolis: Lerner Publications, 2024.

Hammond, Mel. *Women's Professional Basketball.* Minneapolis: Lerner Publications, 2026.

Kendal Coyne Schofield
https://kendallcoyne.com/

PWHL
https://www.thepwhl.com/en/

USA Hockey
https://www.usahockey.com

INDEX

assists, 19, 23, 25–27

defenders, 17, 19–20

forwards, 6, 18–20, 25, 27, 29

goaltenders, 6, 17, 19, 24

most valuable player (MVP), 19, 26

National Women's Hockey League, 9

Olympic medalists, 22, 25, 27

overtime, 5, 18, 20–21

playoffs, 5, 14, 23–24, 26

PWHL Draft, 5, 12, 27

saves, 17, 20, 24

team names, 11

Walter Cup, 4–7, 14, 20, 26

PHOTO ACKNOWLEDGMENTS

Image credits: Troy Parla/Getty Images, pp. 4, 6; AP Photo/Mary Schwalm, p. 7; Gray Mortimore/Allsport/Getty Images, p. 8; Maddie Meyer/Getty Images, p. 9; AP Photo/Jeff Roberson, p. 10; AP Photo/Spencer Colby, p. 12; Monica Schipper/GA/The Hollywood Reporter/Getty Images, p. 13; AP Photo/Rusty Jones/Cal Sport Media, p. 14; AP Photo/Abbie Parr, p. 15; Mark Blinch/Getty Images, p. 16; AP Photo/Frank Gunn/The Canadian Press, p. 17; AP Photo/Andrew Lahodynskyj/The Canadian Press, p. 18; Nick Wosika/Icon Sportswire/Getty Images, p. 19; AP Photo/Christinne Muschi/The Canadian Press, p. 20; Minas Panagiotakis/Getty Images, p. 21; Brandon Magnus/NHLI/Getty Images, p. 22; AP Photo/Graham Hughes/The Canadian Press, p. 23; AP Photo/David Kirouac/Icon Sportswire, p. 25; M. Anthony Nesmith/Icon Sportswire/Getty Images, p. 26; AP Photo/Nick Wosika/Icon Sportswire, p. 28; AP Photo/Mingo Nesmith/Icon Sportswire, p. 29.

Design elements: Vect0r0vich/Getty Images; sarayut Thaneerat/Getty Images; sarayut Thaneerat/Getty Images.

Cover: Steven Garcia/Cal Sport Media via AP Images; Michael Chisholm/Getty Images.